A TEEN'S GUIDE TO
SURVIVING
JUVENILE HALL

Daniel Hernandez

WESTBOW
PRESS®
A DIVISION OF THOMAS NELSON
& ZONDERVAN

WestBow Press books may be ordered through booksellers or by contacting:

WestBow Press
A Division of Thomas Nelson & Zondervan
1663 Liberty Drive
Bloomington, IN 47403
www.westbowpress.com
844-714-3454

Because of the dynamic nature of the Internet, any web addresses or
links contained in this book may have changed since publication and
may no longer be valid. The views expressed in this work are solely those
of the author and do not necessarily reflect the views of the publisher,
and the publisher hereby disclaims any responsibility for them.

Any people depicted in stock imagery provided by Getty Images are
models, and such images are being used for illustrative purposes only.
Certain stock imagery © Getty Images.

ISBN: 978-1-6642-2030-0 (sc)
ISBN: 978-1-6642-2029-4 (hc)
ISBN: 978-1-6642-2031-7 (e)

Library of Congress Control Number: 2021901090

Print information available on the last page.

WestBow Press rev. date: 02/10/2021

CONTENTS

INTRODUCTION

In May 2019, one of Orange County's last functioning boys' camps was closed for good. In actuality, Joplin Youth Center, which was run by the probation department, was a prison tucked away in an obscure canyon in Southern California. Joplin was built in 1956 and housed sixty-four male minors ranging in age from twelve to eighteen. In the old corrections model, there were no cells, as all the boys slept on bunk beds in one large room. Bunk beds lined all four walls. There were no real fences to keep the minors in, but there was a fence at the front gate to stop people from trespassing. Minors occasionally escaped from Joplin, but they always got caught sooner or later. The last five years or so before Joplin closed, the institution housed forty minors due to changes in corrections policies. This number was reduced to thirty-two during Joplin's last two years.

Joplin didn't have any cells, because it was cheaper. In addition, having teens sleeping and working together was much more beneficial to their social development. It was believed teenagers needed socialization and interaction due to their younger ages. For the most part, it worked pretty well. Don't get me wrong—it was a lot of hard work at first. I did have gang rivals sleeping next to one another. On at least two occasions, my group leader and assistant group leader were gang rivals, and they fought each other before arriving at Joplin.

I was hired by the probation department in 2001. Upon completing the six-week-long training class, I was sent to a camp called Los Pinos Conservation Camp as a night staff, meaning I worked the graveyard shift, and I got paid to watch minors sleep. Los Pinos is a camp located in the Cleveland National Forest. The hardest part of that job was trying to stay awake. Luckily, it was for only six months until I got promoted to day staff. I was transferred to Joplin Youth Center. At the time, Joplin was considered the most difficult of all the facilities to work. The minors were rude and disrespectful toward the staff. The veteran staff and supervisors didn't make it any easier. So, in 2002, I was sent to Joplin until my retirement in 2018. With the exception of a few months at juvenile hall, I spent most of my career as a senior juvenile corrections officer at Joplin Youth Center.

You may be asking, *How is he going to give me advice about juvenile hall if he was only there for a few months?* Let's go back to my previous statement about Joplin and how it was considered to be Orange County's most difficult correctional facility. Without a cell to place them in, what do you do with outwardly defiant and violent kids? I had to quickly learn how to recognize behaviors, body language, and other social cues to prevent all sorts of trouble from getting out of control. Ensuring the safety of the staff and minors was a priority at all times. The rules and regulations were the same throughout the corrections system; however, the programs and the physical buildings differed from institution to institution. Remember, there were no cells or rooms to put minors in, so we had to be really creative with how we dealt with the youth.

THE PURPOSE OF THIS BOOK

If you find yourself in the unfortunate situation of sitting in the back of a cop car, handcuffed and heading to juvenile hall, this book may be what you need. This book will give you the tools needed to navigate a bad situation and not make it any worse. This book doesn't mention all the points or models emphasizing change, but it will help. I am not a doctor or a psychologist. I'm just someone with years and years of experience, looking to use my expertise to help others. I have been in stressful situations in which I had nowhere to turn or anyone to trust. It's not like you can Google how to get out of trouble once you're at juvenile hall. But you can read books. I realize that you don't know the staff, and they don't know you. You may feel uncomfortable asking anyone else for help. I get that. This book is another tool you can use to help acclimate to your new surroundings.

There are many youth who were never taught or modeled some of the skills and behaviors mentioned in this book. If you are a minor who finds himself or herself in that category, this book will help you. Most of the research is geared toward helping adults teach kids the skills mentioned in this book. This book will help minors not make a bad situation worse. Ask for help and be patient. You've spent many years developing the behaviors, attitudes, and beliefs that got you in trouble, so change will not happen overnight. It will require practice. Luckily, patience is a skill mentioned in this book.

PATIENCE

I have seen bobcats. The bobcat is a mean looking cat about the size of a medium dog.

Patience is actually quite obvious. When you and your friends get pulled over by the police, the officer may suspect something illegal is going on, such as drinking or the odor of marijuana coming from the car. In that case, you will find yourself sitting on the curb for hours. Patience will be required. While getting booked into juvenile hall, patience is also required. Paperwork has to be completed. Of course, the staff is then required to start a juvenile file on you, if you don't already have one. You will then be searched and cleared by the nurse. Next, you will shower and change clothes. All this could take hours. In the event you are under the influence— let's say Xanax, for example—then it's policy to have the nurse turn you away until you are cleared by a medical doctor. So, back in the police car you go, on your way to an emergency room. Again, this will require you sitting patently at the hospital for hours.

Patience is still required once you get to an intake unit. You are given bedding and hygiene products, which consists of a toothbrush, toothpaste, and deodorant. Then you are assigned a room. After you are given the opportunity to use the restroom, you are escorted to your room, usually by the same person who supervised your bathroom time. And in you go—again for what seems like forever. The staff will then check your file and prepare more papers to go in it. Of course, most of this requires initials and signatures from staff and/or supervisors. Again, more waiting.

These are examples of patience. But how can being patient work in your favor? Easy! Remember: the juvenile hall staff deal with rude and disrespectful teens all the time. For the most part, the staff has been cursed at, disrespected, threatened, and some have even been assaulted. So the old adage that the squeaky wheel gets the oil may not necessarily apply with juvenile hall staff. If you are not familiar with this saying, it means the more you complain, the faster you'll be served. I'm not saying the staff is not going to do their job or violate your rights. But, for example, if there is more than one new person in the unit, the one who is not practicing patience may wait longer than the rest. They have a lot of other young people under their supervision, and safety and security come first. By not being patient, you may come across as needy or problematic. For the safety of other minors and the staff, more staff may be required, which would account for the patience.

Patience is bitter, but its fruit is sweet.

—ARISTOTLE

While working at Joplin, a new minor came into my group. Remember: there were no cells at Joplin. To maintain order, and so the staff could get there paperwork done, all minors were required to remain quiet and lay flat on their beds. This new minor decided to come up to my desk without permission. He asked to use the phone to let his family know he had been transferred to a camp. I informed him the front office staff had already called his family, and he needed to ask permission before coming up to the desk. Needless to say, this minor gave me a look like he couldn't believe I was talking to him like that. He went back to his bed. Approximately five minutes later, I was dealing with a situation with another minor. The new minor, again without permission, came up to my desk and interrupted my conversation with another minor. Already upset and agitated, the minor who I was speaking with was not having it. Needless to say, a fight ensued shortly after.

The new minor could not wait. In short, he had no patience.

HOW TO HAVE PATIENCE IF YOU'RE NOT A PATIENT PERSON

How do you have patience? Parents and adults throw this term around without ever explaining how to have patience. Some teens are physically unable to be patient. Teens with a diagnosis like attention deficit hyperactivity disorder (ADHD) may have difficulty being patient. Patience is a mindset. At one time or another, everyone will lose their patience and may have to remind themselves to relax and take deep breaths. Here are some tips that help.

1. Recognize—recognize that you are not a patient person by nature.
2. Focus—practice being patient; ask yourself if not waiting is worth getting stressed.
3. Relax—once you find yourself getting stressed, take deep breaths and relax.

A few months ago, I was headed to a meeting. I jumped in my car, and I left in plenty of time. Turning right to catch the freeway, traffic was stopped. I again started to become a bit anxious. But I had time, so I thought it was going to be okay. As I moved closer to the freeway, I realized the road was closed, and the police were turning cars around. I was becoming increasingly more impatient as each minute passed. I found myself getting mad, stressed, and very upset because I was now lost and going to be late.

Recognizing my stress level increasing, I took five deep breaths and reminded myself to relax. The person who was involved in the car accident that closed the road was seriously injured or dead, and being late to my appointment paled in comparison.

So put it in perspective. Try to look on the bright side. I know that's what adults say. It truly is a lot easier to say than do. But what are the alternatives? Stress and worry can make you sick. Patience is an important life skill. Most successful people are patient. An example of putting patience into practice is, if the judge gives you thirty days, you can say, "At least I'll get out before summer or winter or the holidays." Things may be bad with your situation, and you may have every right to be impatient. By not showing restraint or patience, things will *not* get better and could possibly get worst. The quote I referenced above by Aristotle means everyone struggles with patience, but the rewards that come with showing patience are well worth the frustration in the end.

WORK

Of course with mountain lions there are
deer, a lot of deer all year around.

Work is not a requirement. Juvenile hall is not a labor camp or a chain gang. While I was working at Joplin, work was required. Not as a form of punishment but for safety reasons. In my seventeen years at the camp, it was evacuated twice due to fires. Staff were stranded twice due to the road being washed out from flooding. So work crews would go out a few times a week to keep the roads cleared of brush, remove fallen trees, and get ready for the rainy season by sandbagging the hillsides to keep the roads open. Chores were completed every day for about fifteen minutes. This, again, was just basic hygiene and cleanliness, throwing out the trash and cleaning the bathrooms. With that being said, there is no such work program like that at juvenile hall. Most units at juvenile hall require you to just to keep your rooms clean. On Saturdays a major cleaning of your room was done. Again, this is for hygiene purposes. You don't know the cleanliness of the last person to sleep on that bed.

There are activities at juvenile hall, but it is mostly boring. Working or volunteering to work helps the time go by a lot faster. Everyone loves a hard worker—someone who can take the initiative and do things without being asked. Even if you don't like juvenile hall, the unit you're in, or even your staff, work helps. One sure way to get the staff off your back is to work. Not only does time go by faster but it usually comes with a positive reward by the staff.

Those who do not work are those minors who usually get in more trouble. But they don't get into trouble for not working. In my experience, those minors who refuse or decline to work do other things to pass the time, such as peer agitation. This just means starting trouble with other minors in the unit. Examples would be trying to pick a fight with others, vandalism, or disrespecting the staff. Working usually helps minors occupy their time. And they don't usually get into trouble.

Don't count the days, Make the days count.

—MUHAMMAD ALI

I had a minor on my caseload who declined every activity. He declined to come out to eat with the rest of the unit, so he ate in his room. He declined to go to school, but he was given a work packet from the school to complete. The minor didn't complete that either. He also declined to shower and clean his room. He received consequences, but that didn't really change his behavior. He got in trouble from the staff and the school. I had to talk to him on a regular basis. I finally got him to at least clean his room and shower regularly.

This example is extreme. Not many minors decline everything, but in this particular case, he suffered from mental health issues. In this instance, he received consequences—not for declining but in the manner he declined. He cursed at the staff and a teacher.

Again, the staff can't make you clean, but time does go by a lot faster. As stated in the above quote by Muhammad Ali, "Don't count the days. Make the days count." While at juvenile hall, and with plenty of time to kill, make your time work for you. I've known kids who learned how to draw while locked up. Others graduated high school early. As the staff and supervisors see that you are attempting to be productive, they are more than willing to help you out. It is a refreshing sight to see a minor wanting to take the initiative to work to improve him or herself.

In some cases, it may never occur to minors to work. Here are tips on how you can look for things to do:

1. You can ask yourself, *What I can do?*
2. Don't always think of yourself.
3. Think outside the box. Don't just wait for things to happen—make positive things happen, like the minor who graduated from high school early. He had nothing but time in his cell and asked his teacher for extra schoolwork, since he wasn't doing anything. That minor graduated from high school a year early.

FOLLOW
DIRECTIONS

There are tons of other animals that I would see regularly such as squirrels, skunks, and foxes. I would see them at night when I would drive home.

Following directions is a big one because it's one of the rules of conduct. Each county has a list of basic rules you have to sign and follow. For example, no fighting, no vandalism, and no escaping. The most general of which is follow directions. Yes, it does sound vague. But no need to worry—you are not going to be asked to do anything difficult, like solve complex math problems. The follow directions rule is more for the safety and security of the youth and staff. This is more of a proactive safety measure. At juvenile hall, you are required to walk with your hands behind your back. You walk in a straight line. You may be asked to not talk to other minors or not speak to minors in a different unit, all of which are for safety reasons. An example of that would be if another minor in your unit decided to attack you. The staff would then yell out to all the remaining minors to get down. The same hypothetical scenario is if a minor did not follow directions. You would need to continue to fight without the staff immediately breaking it up while they waited for other staff to assist. In this example, the two fighters may receive consequences, and the minor who did not get down may be reprimanded for not following directions.

Minors may get a little more upset with staff when this rule is enforced. It's no excuse for the staff to be rude or disrespectful. But the staff will say the same thing over and over again. When giving these directions, the staff may come across as strict. Take it for what it's worth. Don't argue, and always follow directions. Since it is one of the rules of conduct, you can receive minor consequences for breaking this rule. Also, when the court or your probation officer is going to write your progress review for your next court date, calls will go out to your staff, and they will ask how you are doing and if you are following directions.

Everything good that's ever happened to me came out of helping others.

—DANNY TREJO

On a brisk spring morning, I lined up ten youth to collect all the trash around the camp and walk it to the dumpster about a quarter-mile away. After all the trash was collected, I stopped the line of youth who were walking in a single-file line with their hands behind their backs. I informed the group of what we were doing. I instructed them to walk in a single-file line, with both hands behind their backs without talking. There are no sidewalks in the mountains of Joplin, so we walked on the right side of the road. Approximately four minutes into our journey, one youth got out of line again without permission and walked toward a small cluster of rocks and picked something up. Like any good staff member, I yelled out, "Get back in line!"

The youth did not follow my directions. He grabbed something off the rock and walked over toward me. I instructed the rest of the group to stop walking. The other nine minors turned to see what was going on. As the youth approached me with the object in his hand, he stopped in front of me saying, "I think its dead."

Looking down to see what he was showing me, this minor grabbed a baby rattlesnake and placed it in the palm of his hand. I immediately slapped it out of his hand as he repeated again, "It's dead."

Once the snake hit the ground, it uncoiled and slithered away, to the youth's shock and surprise.

In that instance, following directions was important and could have cost that minor his life, or at least a lot of pain and suffering. In his defense, he really enjoyed being at the camp because this was the first time he was ever out of his neighborhood. The youth mentioned above did receive minor consequences for not following directions and dangerous acts, which is also a rule violation. Shortly afterward, he became my group leader.

Like many institutions and agencies, there are several rules and directions to follow. The staff will tell you what to do, not necessarily why.

Following rules is important and will go a long way toward getting the staff to trust you, which does come with its own rewards.

If growing up you were never taught how to follow directions, or it was never enforced, just know that at juvenile hall this is one rule you will definitely need to follow:

1. Listen to what you are instructed to do.
2. Do it.

RESPECT

Southern California is prone to brush fires during fire season. In my time at Joplin the camp was evacuated twice.

Why respect? The basic mentality among kids from the neighborhood is "F" them. They're the cops. They don't care about me, and they want me to get in trouble. For the most part, this is not true. Until you got arrested and are escorted into juvenile hall, you are unknown to the staff. They don't know you, and you are not important enough for the staff to lose sleep over. They didn't arrest you. They didn't tell you to rob or shoot anyone. If you don't know the staff, it's easy to assume the staff doesn't like you or the staff is out to get you. It is much easier to be disrespectful or come across as disrespectful to people you don't know. The juvenile hall staff are like anyone else—some people you really like, and others you can't stand.

You should use your experience at juvenile hall as a learning moment. For example, consider your boss. If you do not like your boss's personality, or if you don't like him or her as a person, that is fine. But don't disrespect them because of it. You may find yourself out of a job. So how does being respectful translate to succeeding at juvenile hall? Let's look at the definition in *Merriam-Webster*: "respect—to be considered worthy of high regard." I am most definitely not saying this. Just don't be mean or disrespectful for no reason.

Being respectful in juvenile hall does come with rewards. Let me clarify: rewards that may come in a different form than what you expect. For being nice you will not get out early or reduced charges, anything like that. But for being respectful you may get to assist staff in certain projects. A minor who is respectful to the staff and others usually has proven they can be trusted with small tasks for the most part. So you may then get to miss population verification, go on field trips or sit in when a guest speak comes in. Again, juvenile hall is extremely boring, and these activities help the time go by faster.

Make improvements, not excuses.
Seek respect, not attention.

—ROY T. BENNETT

One late afternoon I was working a different shift and in a different group. The staff member working behind me was a very smart longtime veteran. A new minor who had been there about a week was acting up and getting into trouble. The other kids in the group didn't care for him. The minor was calling out without permission and appeared to be on the verge of yelling. The staff member called the minor over to have a seat in the chair next to the desk. In a calm and respectful tone, the staff member thanked the minor, saying, "Because of you, I'm a better person, so thank you."

The quote above means strive to better yourself, and don't make excuses for why you failed at something. Also, seek respect of those who are worthy of your respect and not attention. Those who just seek attention are usually always bad. The little kid running around the department store causing trouble is seeking attention.

The staff member was on the verge of losing his temper. He did not show any disrespect to the minor, even though the other staff and other minors in the group wanted him to. Showing respect to others, even when they don't deserve it, gives you more self-respect. This goes a long way toward showing others you are a person of character. To be respectful is an indication of who you are as a person. If you were never taught how to be respectful, it's never too late to learn.

1. Find someone who you respect and follow their example.
2. Stay calm. People who never learned respect think people are disrespecting them, and this is more than likely not the case.
3. Have an open mind. Don't be so quick to lose your temper by thinking you're being disrespected.
4. Be polite. Respectful people are usually polite and say please and thank you.

TEAMWORK

The rock four minors and I moved
on a special work crew.

You may be asking, *Why teamwork?* Remember: juvenile hall is really boring. Even though you come out to participate in different activities during the day, it's when the staff want you to come out or if it's on the schedule for the day. That means a lot of waiting around. These are guidelines to help manage getting through juvenile hall as easily and painlessly as possible.

When I say teamwork, that doesn't mean you have to like everyone in your unit. I'm just saying play nice to reduce the consequences given to the entire unit. An example of this would be if there was a fight while the group was on free time, and all the minors were out of their rooms watching TV. The first thing the staff will do is yell out, "Get down," meaning everyone lay facedown on the floor, and then the staff will break up the fight. Once the fighters are secured, you are instructed to get up and go into your rooms while the investigation is started and reports are written. This could take an entire shift. Needless to say, you will be in your room for a long time. Did I mention juvenile hall is really boring? In short, if you have a rival or do not get along with someone, I suggest you wait until you are released. The easiest thing to do is not talk to that person, and do your best to stay away from them.

Yes, it may sound weird, but your unit is like a team. Of course, the staff can divide you, meaning they'll bring half out or a few minors at a time. If one minor is getting into trouble, and the rest of the group is minding their own business, then just that kid will get into trouble. If the staff knows two or three kids are acting up, they will get into trouble. The issue escalates when the staff doesn't know who's causing problems in the unit. The restrooms at juvenile hall get inspected daily—sometimes twice a day—for vandalism. So, if the restroom was recently vandalized, then the staff will conduct an investigation, which will affect the entirety of the unit. It is unfair that the entire unit will get into trouble, but again, this is for the safety of all the minors in the unit.

Alone we can do so little, together we can do so much.

—HELEN KELLER

One very hot summer day, a group of five minors and I were tasked with moving a very large boulder that was next to the road. Work trucks were having a difficult time getting the vehicles around the rock along the road, so the powers that be asked if I could take a work crew out to move the rather large rock. We grabbed tools such as shovels and steel pry bars, and we attempted to roll the rock down the hill. After approximately five minutes, I thought it was hopeless—the rock didn't budge an inch. There was one youth who said, "I have an idea." He positioned us into place and instructed us on what to do. With teamwork and a great deal of effort, the rocked moved. This gave us hope. We communicated and worked together, and an hour later the two-thousand-pound rock was out of the way and on the other side of the road. Months later, the youths on that work crew would brag and beam with pride, saying to anyone who would listen, "We moved that rock."

The best units in juvenile hall are full of minors who work together. It may be as easy as sitting and quietly minding your own business.

Teamwork is just like any team sport—soccer,

basketball, or baseball. You need to work together toward a common goal. There is no difference at juvenile hall. Behave in a way that does not make the entire unit get in trouble. These tips may come in handy:

1. Watch someone who you feel is a positive example, and try to follow that person's lead.

2. Practice. How do you do that in juvenile hall? Engage in activities in which you are working together with someone and not playing against someone. For example, in cards or chess, you're playing against someone. If you are building a puzzle, you're working with someone to complete a common goal.

3. Patience. They may not do things the way you do. It's not wrong—just different. Be patient.

4. Relax. Working together can be enjoyable. It's still work, but if you were doing it alone, it could take twice as long. Relax and enjoy the help.

COMMUNICATION

Usually a staff spots a mountain lion
at least once a year. In the 17 years I
worked there I had never seen one.

Communication is a very important skill in and out of juvenile hall. Remember: the staff does not really know you, and they deal with hundreds of kids every day. So, if you can communicate properly, that will be key to your success. What does that mean? Juvenile hall is a structured environment. Things are run on a schedule, and there is a time and a place for everything. If you have personal issues, raise your hand and wait patiently to be called on. Ask if you may approach the staff; then ask your question and wait for the response in its entirety. Do not call out, and do your best to not get upset or frustrated.

In my experience, communication is a trait that seems to be the most difficult for some to master. There are some minors who never learned how to communicate effectively. These are also the same minors who have never been told no. I had kids in my group who would just come up to me without permission and start yelling out their demands. A good majority of these demands were out of my control. Minors who enter juvenile hall for the first time usually exhibit these characteristics. More often than not, the staff won't view these issues as life or death. If you can calmly communicate your needs or concerns to the staff, your request will more than likely be granted if possible.

Along with communication is listening. Most minors stop listening if they feel their request won't be granted. You should stay focused and truly listen. Ask for an explanation if you don't understand the response. Minors who never learned to listen have a tendency to get into more arguments. An example would be if you were to get into an argument with a friend; then five minutes later you're friend asked you for a favor. How likely are you to grant him that request?

> *Wise men speak because they have something to say; fools because they have to say something.*
>
> —PLATO

One afternoon I received a new intake into my group. Approximately one hour earlier, there was a fight. The majority of the staff was busy finishing up reports and getting together files and other important pieces of information. As the minor was escorted into my group, I pointed to his bed and had an experienced youth assist him in making his bed. The youth placed his linen on his bed, and without permission he made his way up to my desk. I was filling out paperwork with one of the youths involved in the fight. I instructed the new minor to continue to make his bed, and once I was done, I would be more than happy to assist him. The youth then started talking and making demands that he needed to speak to the supervisor in charge. After a brief argument, I called the supervisor over the radio and informed him that a youth wanted to speak with him. The supervisor stated that he should have a seat, and he will speak with him as soon as possible. Forty-five minutes later, once all the safety concerns were addressed, the youth was met by the supervisor. The youth was upset and became argumentative and disrespectful toward the supervisor. At this point, that youth received consequences for making threats toward the supervisor.

Unfortunately, that minor walked into an unpleasant situation. As you can see, he did not communicate properly. As a result of not communicating and listening, he got upset and received some consequences. Believe it or not, the safety of the staff and youth in the facility were very important, and the gang tension in the institution was very high at that time. That youth was unable to recognize this, and he didn't seem to care. He never asked the supervisor his question, which got him in trouble.

What if you were never taught how to communicate properly?

1. Think of what you are going to say and how you're going to say it.
2. Wait for the right time.
3. Wait for the right place.

4. Say what you want to say.

5. Listen to the response—really listen to the response.

6. Ask questions if the answer is unclear or if you don't understand.

INITIATIVE

There are tones of rattlesnakes at Joplin. I
have seen more than my share of snakes.

What is initiative? *Webster's* definition is as follows: "the ability to assess and initiate things independently." Basically, it means doing something without being told. It may sound strange or weird. In the context of being successful in juvenile hall, it means anything positive. A few examples would be your homework. Sometime certain programs assign homework and extra work assignments. To take the initiative would be to look for a work assignment and ask if you could clean before you're asked. While you are at school, ask for work you can take back to the unit. These are examples of taking the initiative.

Stephen Richards, a professor of criminal justice, for example. Stephen Richards spent nine years in prison for selling drugs. While he was locked up, he received a bachelor's degree, then a master's degree from the University of Wisconsin, and then his PhD from Iowa State University. After his release from prison, he became a professor of criminal justice at the University of Wisconsin. There is also Isaac Wright Jr., who was wrongfully accused of selling drugs and was sentenced to life in prison. While in prison, he went to school to become a paralegal. He helped get his case overturned. He continued to go to school and received a law degree. He is currently working as a lawyer.

Both of these men took the initiative to do something with the time they had. They made time work for them, and they did not let time slip away. So, if you find yourself at juvenile hall with time to burn, make that time work for you. Graduate from high school early. Enroll in college classes. If school is not your thing, become a better artist if you already know how to draw or paint. Find what interests you and learn all you can. If you have no idea of what interests you or what you would like to do as a career, ask the staff. Take that time to discover your interests. Most of the staff where either in the military or had gone to college. Try asking them what there major was and ask them what they learned. For example, my major was sociology. When minors ask me, they usually respond with, "Oh." I know they have no idea what sociology is, so I use this as a teachable moment.

I would rather regret the things I have done than the things I have not.

—LUCILLE BALL

I had a minor in my group who I had known for many years. He had been in and out of custody for years. He learned over time to use his time productively. During his free time, he would continually exercise. When he was in his room, he would lie on his bed and read books. He always applied himself and completed his assignments during his program hour. He graduated from high school early. When he wasn't reading, he was drawing. He was a pretty good artist.

This minor took the initiative and asked his teachers if he could take schoolwork back to the unit. He would also ask the teachers if he could do extra credit. This helped him graduate from high school early. While the group was out watching a movie, he would ask the staff if he could quietly do push-ups and sit-ups in the corner.

The quote above encourages readers to take action. If it doesn't work out, at least you tried. Anyone can do nothing. In order to take the initiative, simply get started. If you know you're going to have to move a mountain of dirt, don't wait until the last minute. Without being told, pick up the shovel and get started. You are going to have to do it anyway.

The same also applies to getting off probation. For example, if one of your conditions is to go to school in order to not receive a violation, then go to school.

How do you take the initiative if you have never been taught?

1. Think about what needs to be done.
2. Ask, "What can I do?"
3. Ask someone if you can do that, like a staff member or a teacher.
4. Do it.

It should be noted that this skill may require practice for some people. There are a lot of minors at juvenile hall who don't know how to ask to take work to the unit. Most teachers at juvenile hall do not assign homework. Think outside the box and help yourself, since you have the time.

PARTICIPATE

Twice at my time at Joplin during two bad winter storms which caused rocks and mud to cover the road, trapping the staff at the camp making them pull a 24 hour shift.

Participation is a tool to help pass time and even help you learn something. I have said before that while at juvenile hall all units are required to do a program. This occurs every day without fail. If you participate, it will make time go by faster. Participation also applies to other things, such as schoolwork, programs, and everything else. What is everything else? The staff can't make you do anything you do not want to do, but you also can't do whatever you want. You can decline almost anything, but then you are going to spend more time in your room. For example, the staff will ask you if you want to come out to watch a movie. If you say no, you will just stay in your room. Of course, you may receive consequences for declining certain things, but you don't have to do anything you don't want to do. You can decline your daily exercise. You can decline to shower. You can decline to go to school, and you can decline to see the nurse. But these decisions have consequences. For example, if you decline school, you will not get credit for school. If you decline to see the nurse, and you have a medical condition, that puts you in jeopardy. In that event, you may have to go to the emergency room again, which is another long and unpleasant day.

Most things in life are a choice. One choice may be more favorable than the other. Some choices are more difficult than others. Our choices are dictated by many factors, such as friends, money, and information. A lot of teens are in juvenile hall for trying to impress their friends by going along with a foolish idea. Money again is a factor that guides are choices. You may think, *Does my family have the money to hire a lawyer, or do I go with the public defender?*

To participate or not participate is a choice. Do you want to make the best of the time you have? A wise man said, "Anyone can do nothing—it requires no special gifts or talent."

> *Do more than belong: participate. Do more than care: help. Do more than believe: practice. Do more than be fair: be kind. Do more than forgive: forget. Do more than dream: work.*
>
> —WILLIAM ARTHUR WARD

At juvenile hall and other correctional institutions, there are no shortages of really talented artist. Joplin High School would host a function to display students' writings and artwork to high-ranking county officials. There was one minor in my group who was a good artist but did not want to enter the school's art contest. It just wasn't cool. Finally, he decided to participate after some coxing. This minor drew a face with a pencil. One of the judges was so impressed with the drawing. He showed it to a friend of his, who asked if he could purchase the drawing. Due to this minor's participation, this minor won the contest, sold his drawing for fifty dollars, and was offered an art scholarship after his release.

Participating is no guarantee of anything great or wonderful. But by not participating, I can guarantee nothing will change.

A lot of teens don't like to be called on at school to participate. For example, they don't like to be called on to read. Sometimes reading out loud is embarrassing. To participate, you are opening yourself up to something that may be uncomfortable. Again, these are tools to help you better yourself. To succeed at juvenile hall—and in life—you may need to be uncomfortable. Learning new things is never an easy process, and it will usually pay off in the long run one way or another.

How to participate:

1. Have the right attitude. Be prepared to be uncomfortable.
2. Be open to the experience.
3. Do it.

OPEN MIND

I do not mind any of the wild life on the mountain. But tarantulas really creep me out and in August during mating season these supersize spiders were everywhere.

Being open-minded goes with participation. Coming into juvenile hall, there are some minors who are extremely intelligent and quite knowledgeable in many subjects. There are other minors who have just stopped going to school or are two or three grades behind where they should be. In either case, they may hold on to faulty beliefs or perceptions. I recall a conversation in which two youths got into a very heated conversation over who was correct regarding a historical fact. Listening to this conversation, I was in awe of how passionate those two were about being right. They almost came to blows over their discussion. They both had the good sense to ask me. I informed them that they were both wrong and got upset at each other for no reason. I would intentionally show black-and-white movies to my group in order to expose them to something new. Most minors will request to see gang movies, movies about cars, or movies with action. By putting on a black-and-white movie, I would hear the usual groans, then silence as the minors asked me questions about the plot or characters in the movie. The groans reflected close-minded thinking. They assumed the movie was going to be boring and that they wouldn't like it. Of course, by the time the movie was over, most minors would request to see it again.

One of my duties was to complete special work assignments. Again, more moaning and complaining about having to work. The group did a lot of brush clearing and weeding to prevent seasonal fires. We also sandbagged roads in the winter to prevent flooding. As I instructed my group to get ready to work, the most common thought was that Joplin made minors work as a form of punishment. I explained to the group that the camp had been evacuated twice during my seventeen-year tenure due to fires. Once the minors understood this, they were more open-minded and worked a lot harder. They usually did a good job.

Before you start to argue with the staff or complain, keep an open mind. There may be reasons or information you do not know.

Without an open-mind, you can never be a great success.

—MARTHA STEWART

While in my thirties and forties, I had friends who thought it would be fun to go skydiving. I had always thought it was probably the dumbest thing anyone could do. First of all, I really don't like going on roller coasters, so I figured I would never go skydiving. Then I turned fifty, and two of my sons thought it would be fun. They asked if I would go with them. I didn't immediately say no, but I said I would think about it. I did some research and talked to people who had done it, and I thought I really never gave it a chance. There are thousands of people who have tried it for the first time every year. I decided to be open-minded and do something new. In my fifties, I jumped out of an airplane. It is a positive memory that my son and I will always cherish. If I were close-minded, that experience would have been lost forever.

If you find yourself in the same trouble, doing the same things over and over again, you need to break that cycle. To be successful, open your mind to ideas and concepts that are new and different. Nothing will change unless you make it change. Open your mind; your thoughts control your emotions and actions.

Remember that having an open mind is not the same as being impulsive. Having an open mind is giving ideas a chance in order to think about them. An example is not immediately rejecting a staff member's idea. Having an open mind is giving the idea merit and looking into it yourself.

How to be open-minded:

1. Patience—don't be so eager to say no. Give it a chance until you can think about it.

2. Try—give it a chance until you decide you don't like it. Don't assume you won't like it until you try.

3. Practice—you may be used to automatically saying no. Having an open mind may take practice.

SELF-CONTROL

During Tarantula mating season once a year you will see these huge wasps flying around looking, for Tarantulas they are also know as tarantula hawks. They could probably cover the palm of your hand.

Self-control is a really important characteristic to have in and out of juvenile hall. In any book you read on how to succeed in life, in business, or in school, somewhere on the list will be self-control. For many years, mental health professionals have labeled teens as having poor impulse control. What does that mean? It means that as soon as you have an impulse—idea, thought, or feeling—you need to act on it immediately. Not all teens, but in my experience, there are many in juvenile hall who do not have any self- control. The experts do know what they are talking about. The minors who don't have self-control are usually pretty easy to spot. Some tend to be more immature than the rest of the minors in the unit. Most of the minors who have no self-control get into trouble more often than rest of the minors in the unit.

Impulse control, or a lack of self-control, is

usually taught at an early age. If you are in juvenile hall, and you still have no self-control, more than likely you have not learned or seen it modeled by adults, parents, or other teens. Do not fear—it's not the end of the world. First of all, recognize that you do not have any self-control. Once an idea come to you, do you find a way to make it happen regardless of the consequences? For example, you want a new pair of shoes, and you don't have the money to buy them. You know your parents don't have the money, so you either steal them or steal the money from an innocent person to buy them. The keys to gaining self-control are structure. Luckily for you, most juvenile institutions have tons of structure. What is structure? Structure is a behavioral routine and being instructed on your behavioral expectations.

At juvenile hall, you follow a set schedule every

day, and the schedule doesn't change too often. Besides fallowing a schedule, you are structured or informed of your behavioral expectations for each activity. For example, when you are about to do a line movement, the staff will tell you, "I will line you up, and you will line up quietly in a single-file line, with your hands behind your back without talking." The staff will then proceed to line up the group. The staff does this for every activity. During breakfast, the staff will communicate behavioral expectations for the day. A minor who lacks self-control will not like the schedule or the structure, and once a different idea pops into his mind, and he decides to alter the schedule or behavioral expectation, that minor will then receive consequences. Corrective behavior is another way to learn self-control. At juvenile hall, this system is built in to the basic rules when giving consequences. Youths are told why they are being disciplined. Most youths usually know what they did was wrong and are prepared to handle the consequences. Over time, these youths will develop self-control. This type of self-control is crucial to being successful in juvenile hall.

*One's greatest challenge
is to control oneself.*

—KAZI SHAMS

One summer day I worked a day I didn't usually work—a Sunday-morning shift. Since this shift was new to me, the staff were being kind and had me work visiting. This required me to check in parents and search their bags. It had been years since I worked visiting, but the procedure was the same. I picked two well-behaved and respected minors to help out. We carried the visiting supplies to the visiting area, which was approximately two acres outside with a beautiful view overlooking the canyon. I instructed one youth to set things up. The other youth ran toward the far end of the visiting area, setting up things on picnic benches. The other youth turned to me, saying, "Indio, that's messed up."

I turned to him with a puzzled look. He then gestured to the other minor. Immediately, it dawned on me. These two were gang rivals, I apologized to him and sent him back to his group. Both minors were mature and had a great deal of self-control. Their immediate response was to fight or disrespect one another.

I got along with both kids, and if it wasn't for a line on some street separating their gangs, those two would probably be the best of friends. They both exhibited self-control in how they handled the situation. They could have fought, they could have disrespected each other's gangs, or they could have misbehaved. They decided to bring it to my attention, knowing it was an honest mistake on my part. They had a great deal to lose if they acted on their impulses, but they chose not to. I apologized to both minors, and we joked about it afterward—separately, of course.

How can you develop self-control if it's not natural, or you have never been taught self-control?

1. Structure—make a schedule and make a plan to stick to it. Things will come up to change this from time to time, but try to keep to a schedule.

2. Model—look at others to see if they have self-control and attempt to copy them.

3. Think—making goals helps. Most successful people write out their goals and strive to complete them. This could be long-term and short-term goals.

Note:

Long-term goals—examples would be getting off probation, graduating from high school, going to college, or starting a business.

Short-term goals—examples include going to school every day, staying off drugs for one day, or applying for one job by the end of the week.

CONCLUSION

The purpose of writing this book is to open your mind to the way things are. It should be noted that not all counties operate in the same way. Things always differ from state to state and from county to county. This is a compilation of my experiences in working at three juvenile institutions over two decades. This list does not stop at these ten points. There are tons of other skills and behaviors and other variables we could get into. These are general points of interests. True success stems from individual to individual. And other factors, such as mental health issues, substance abuse, and a support system influence an individual's trajectory. A support system is someone who will encourage and help you when needed. For example, I met a mother who preferred her son being locked up. She said it was safer for him. In this example, the mother often called the minor's probation officer, hoping her son would get sent back to juvenile hall.

The ten points in the book are usually taught when you're young. Somewhere down the line, a step was missed. That doesn't mean you will never be successful, or you are doomed to be locked up for the rest of your life. It means these things need to be worked on and mastered. I strongly believe everyone should continue to work on themselves and better themselves a little every day. You can do this through education or by setting goals for yourself. Chip away at these goals a little bit every day or every week. If you find this too difficult because of outside influences, ask for help or ask someone for directions. Those who suffer from mental health issues should ask for help. Some recourse include the internet, school, or churches. The same applies to individuals struggling with drug addiction. At juvenile hall, there are mental health experts, substance abuse counselors, and pastors and priests. You do not need to wait to be locked up to take advantage of these resources. They apply all over—you just need to ask for the help.

There is always a way if you want it bad enough. Remember: You are the only one who can change you. Do the work. I can tell you how, but I cannot do it for you.

BIBLIOGRAPHY

Stevenson, Tom. "6 Quotes by Aristotle That Will Change Your Life Forever." Mind Café, May 5, 2020. https://medium.com/mind-cafe/6-quotes-by-aristotle-that-will-change-your-life-forever-f3e7b0394e36.

Elaine. "Don't count the days. Make the days count." Pass it On, September 20, 2016. https://www.passiton.com/inspirational-quotes/4005-dont-count-the-days-make-the-days-count.

Rodenhizer, Samuel. "Everything good." Quotation Celebration, September 9, 2018. https://www.quotationcelebration.wordpress.com.

Bennett, Roy T. "The Light in the Heart." Goodreads, 26 February 26, 2016. https://www.goodreads.com/book/show/29359991-the-light-in-the-heart.

Keller, Helen. "American Foundation for the Blind." American Foundation for the Blind, June 28, 2018. https://www.afb.org/blog/entry/happy-birthday-helen.

Zwicky, Arnold. "The wise talk because they have something to say." Language Log, November 2, 2008. https://languagelog.ldc.upenn.edu/nll/?p=796.

Regretful Tea Drinker. "Things I Could Have Done Better, A Life Time of Regrets." Things I Could Have Done Better, August 2, 2015. https://thingsicouldhavedonebetter.word-press.com/2015/08/02/o-world/#:~:text=August%202%2C%202015-,I'd%20rather%20regret%20the%20things%20I've%20done%2C,on%20something%20good%20later%20on.

Love of Life. "Do more than belong." Love of Life Quotes, September 29, 2015. https://loveoflifequotes.com/motivational/william-arthur-ward-do-more-than-belong-participate/.

Strong Woman Quotes. "Without an open-minded mind, you can never be a great success." Strong Woman Quotes, August 10, 2019. https://strongwomenquotes.com/without-an-open-minded-mind-you-can.

Bazzastotle. "One's Greatest Challenge Is to Control Oneself." Bazzastotle, Bazzastotle, March 19, 2017. https://bazzastotle.com/2017/03/19/ones-greatest-challenge-is-to-control-oneself.

ABOUT THE AUTHOR

Daniel Hernandez is a retired juvenile corrections officer who spent seventeen years working at two camps in the hills of Southern California and at Juvenile Hall. This is his first book.

NOTES

NOTES

NOTES

NOTES

NOTES

NOTES

NOTES

NOTES

9 781664 220300